THIS LITTLE LAND
Menke Katz

Translations by Rivke Katz & Aaron Kramer

Cover Illustration by Rivke Katz
Text Illustrations by Bebe Barkan

Jewish Writers Chapbook 1
Series Editor: Stanley H. Barkan

Cross-Cultural Communications
Merrick, New York
1992

Copyright © 1992 by Cross-Cultural Communications
Yiddish and English poetry originals Copyright © 1965, 1970, 1972, 1991 by Menke Katz
English translations Copyright © 1982, 1991 by Menke Katz, Rivke Katz, and Aaron Kramer
Cover illustration Copyright © 1982, 1992 by Rivke Katz
Text illustrations Copyright © 1982, 1992 by Bebe Barkan
Back cover photograph Copyright © 1980 by Chris Farlekas
All rights reserved under International Copyright Conventions. Except for brief passages quoted in a newspaper, magazine, radio, or television review, no part of this book may be reproduced in any form or by any means, electronic or mechanical, including photocopying and recording, or by any information storage and retrieval system, without permission in writing from the publisher.

The Yiddish poems in this chapbook first appeared in the first section, "Dos Kleyneke Land" (This Little Land), of *Tsfat* (Tel-Aviv: I. L. Peretz, 1979). Many of the original English-language poems were previously published in newspapers, magazines, and books, including the following: *The New York Herald Tribune, The New York Times, Trapani Nuova* (Sicily); *The Atlantic Monthly, Commentary, Fiddlehead* (Canada), *Harper's Bazaar, Home Planet News, Manifold* (England), *Poet* (India), *Poet Lore, Prairie Schooner, Sewanee Review, South and West, The Smith; Burning Village, International Festival of Poetry & Art/1973, The Land of Manna, Rockrose.*

The editors and publishers of the above are gratefully acknowledged. Special thanks to Harry Smith for numerous selections from *Rockrose* and *Burning Village.*

We are also grateful to the New York State Council on the Arts and the National Endowment for the Arts whose seed grants, in part, have made this publication possible.

The **CROSS-CULTURAL REVIEW JEWISH WRITERS CHAPBOOK SERIES** features, in the words of Isaac Bashevis Singer, Jewish writers, not just writers who happen to be Jewish. This series is part of the CROSS-CULTURAL REVIEW SERIES OF WORLD LITERATURE AND ART IN SOUND, PRINT, AND MOTION, and is, thus, usually available in palm-sized and regular paperback and clothbound, limited and boxed editions, as well as audiocassette and videocassette. All submissions should be preceded by a query letter and accompanied by an S.A.S.E. All rights in copy matter will be treated as unconditionally assigned for publication to Cross-Cultural Communications, though copyright reverts to authors, translators, graphic and performing artists upon publication.

All orders and correspondence should be addressed to the publisher:
Cross-Cultural Communications, 239 Wynsum Avenue, Merrick, N.Y. 11566-4725/U.S.A.
Telephone: (516) 868-5635. Fax: (516) 379-1901.
Series Editor: Stanley H. Barkan. *Art Editor:* Bebe Barkan, *Editorial Board:* Karen Alkalay-Gut, Enzo Bonventre, Jozo Boškovski, Laura Boss, Joseph Bruchac, Siv Cedering, Flavia Cosma, Roy Cravzow, David Curzon, Nicolò D'Alessandro, Enid Dame, Arthur Dobrin, Ruth Feldman, Nancy Festinger, David Gershator, Phillis Gershator, Maria Mazziotti Gillan, Talât S. Halman, Leo Hamalian, J. C. Hand, Gunnar Harding, Steven Hartman, Rose Graubart Ignatow, Maria Jacketti, Kahionhes, Ko Won, José Kozer, Aaron Kramer, Barbara Lekatsas, Donald Lev, Manuel van Loggem, Branko Mikasinovich, Marilyn Mohr, Janet Morgan, Raymond R. Patterson, Ritva Poom, Gregory Rabassa, Mindy Rinkewich, Charlz Rizzuto, Georgine Sanders, Nat Scammacca, Nina Scammacca, Saverio A. Scammacca, Linda Scheer, Sheryl St. Germain, Lou Stevens, Nikki Stiller, Brian Swann, Adam Szyper, Alfred Van Loen, Vantzeti Vassilev, Boris Vishinski, Nikola Vizner, Zoran Vragolov, Leo Vroman, Hans van de Waarsenburg, Claire Nicolas White, Joost de Wit.

First Edition
Cross-Cultural Review Jewish Writers Chapbook 1
ISSN 0271-6070
Regular Editions
ISBN 0-89304-325-7 Clothbound/ISBN 0-89304-326-5 Paperback
Limited Edition
ISBN 0-89304-329-6
Palm-sized Editions
ISBN 0-89304-327-3 Clothbound/ISBN 0-89304-328-1 Paperback
Designed by Bebe Barkan
Printed in the United States of America

For my father Heershe-David, my mother Badane,
my wife Rivke, my daughter Troim, my son Heershe-David,
my brothers Elchik, Berke, Yeiske, Meishke
my sister Bloomke—
who always inspired me to love life more,
to believe that ages beyond me will not forget me.

—Forever, your Menke

NOTE: Menke Katz writes in both Yiddish and English. He does not, however, translate his own poetry since he prefers "to write new poems." The one translation of Menke by Menke included in this chapbook is a great exception.

דער ערשטער רעגן

דער ערשטער רעגן, דאָס געזאַנג פֿון האַרבסט, זינגט פֿון שפּע אין פֿעלד.
ערשטע וואַסערלעך אײַלן אַ ניַיעם מזל אָנצוזאָגן,
שװענקען אַזױעק איטלעך דורשט פֿון לאַנגן זומער אין מיטן טאָג:
שמעקט מיט פֿראַצע פֿון מענטש, מיט האָניק פֿון בלום, מיט ברכות פֿון פֿעלד.
אַ פּשוטע בריק פֿון װאַר צו חלום, פֿון הימל צו ערד,
פֿאַלן איבעריקע שאָטנס פֿון קרומע דורות, קעגן טאָג.
בלומען נאָכן ערשטן רעגן, װי כּלות אױסגעצװאָגן.
אַ טראָפֿן רעגן איז אַ קוש פֿון גינגאָלד אין געבענטשטן פֿעלד.

THE FIRST RAIN

The first rain, autumn's song, sings of abundance in the field.
First rivulets rush to announce a better fate,
rinse off the long summer's thirst in the heat of day:
fragrant with human toil, the honey of flower, the blessing of field.
A simple bridge from heaven to earth, from dream to reality,
useless shadows from warped eras fall against the day.
Like spruced-up brides are the flowers after the first rain.
A drop of rain is a golden kiss in the blessed field.

Translated by Aaron Kramer

אַ מאַראַנץ

איך האָב היַינט צום ערשטן מאָל, אין ארץ ישראל,
אַ פּשוטן מאַראַנץ אויף אַ בוים געזען,
האָב איך דעם ערשטן מאַראַנץ, אין ארץ ישראל,
ווי גאָטס ערשטן באַשאַף, ווי ליכט פון בראשית דערזען.

מיט אַזאַ ציטער האָב איך צום ערשטן מאָל, אין ניו-יאָרק,
אויף די שטיינער פון דעלענסי סטריט אַן ערשטן קוש פאַרזוכט.
מיט אַזאַ ניַיגער האָט אָדם הראשון דערהערט חוהס קול,
געצאַלט מיט גן-עדן פאַר דעם טעם פון אַן ערדישער פרוכט.

דעם מאַראַנץ האָב איך ווי מיט אייביקע פינגער געריסן,
ווי פּלוצעם וואַלט פון בוים אַן עץ החיים געוואָרן.
דער מאַראַנץ, ווי צו דער זון, אַ קיַילעכדיקער שליסל,
צו עפענען אַלע מזלות פון געבענטשטע יאָרן.

גאָר דאָס ליכט פון "באחרית הימים" ליַיכט אונדז אַנטקעגן,
וועט נאָך ירושלים פאַריאָגן סדום פון גאָר דער ערד,
וועט נאָך ישעיה הנביא אויף אייביק צעברעכן די שווערד,
וועט נאָך בליַיבן פון גן-עדן: אַ העלער, ערדישער וועג.

לחיים ייִדן!
ס'וועט שוין קיין חושך פון נעכטן אונדזער מאָרגן ניט פאַרוואָרן.
ייִדן מיט ריחות פון פריש-צעאַקערטער מדבר-ערד,
ייִדן מיט דער ליכטיקייט פון אברהמס אַלע שטערן,
ווי דעם מאַראַנץ איז זאַפט און פרייד און זעט מיַין פאַלק באַשערט.

ס'האָט מיר היַינט צום ערשטן מאָל, ארץ ישראל,
אַ פּשוטן מאַראַנץ אין אַ פּרדס געגעבן.
כ'האָב היַינט צום ערשטן מאָל, אין ארץ ישראל,
געמאַכט שהחיינו איבערן לעבן.

AN ORANGE

Today, for the first time in Israel,
I saw a simple orange on a tree.
The first orange I beheld in Israel
seemed like God's first gem, like the light of Genesis, to me.

Just so tremulous, in New York, I received
my first kiss on the stones of Delancey Street.
Just so curious, Adam heard the call of Eve,
bartered Eden for the taste of a fruit, earth-sweet.

As if with immortal fingers, I tore the orange free—
as if, all of a sudden, this had become
God's Tree; as if its orange were the sun's round key
for opening all the blessed years to come.

Before us the light of the End of Days will shine,
Jerusalem will yet drive Sodom from the earth,
Isaiah will yet break the sword for all time—
Eden will yet leave us a bright earthly path.

L'chaim, Yidn!
Yesterday's gloom won't block the dawn that is ours—
Jews with the scent of fresh-ploughed desert earth—
Jews with the radiance of all Abraham's stars ...
Like the orange, my people are destined for life and feast and mirth.

Today, in an orchard, for the first time, Israel
gave me a simple orange as a gift.
Today, for the first time, in Israel
I thanked God for having lived.

Translated by Aaron Kramer

אַ פֿאַרלאָזטער װײַנגאָרטן

ניט געקליבענע טרויבן רינען אויס אַליין אין װײַנען,
טרינקען אָן מיט צײַטיקייט דער עקרהדיקער ערד,
איז די טרויבן נאָר די נעגל פֿונעם דאָרן באַשערט.
אַ לעצטער שטראַל דערמאָנט זיך אָן די פֿאַרגעסענע װײַנען,
גלעט אויס מיט אייגענעם טויט, מיט העלסטן סוף יעדע פּײַן,
איז די טרויבן װי דורך אַ שפּיגל, אַ לעצטער קוש באַשערט.
די נאַכט שמעקט מיט אומקום פֿון אויסגערונענע װײַנען.
די שיפֿרות פֿון װײַנטרויבן װערט דאָס געװיין פֿון דער ערד.

A DESERTED VINEYARD

Unharvested grapes ooze themselves out into wines,
drenching the barren earth with mellowness;
the nails of the thorn will be a wine-press.
The sun's last ray recalls the forgotten wines,
soothes every pain with its own death, radiantly dies
pledging the grapes, as through a mirror, one last kiss.
The night reeks with the death of oozed-out wines.
The intoxication of winegrapes turns to earthcries.

Translated by Aaron Kramer

אָוונט אין צפת

אר״י הקדוש אין קילקײַט פֿון אָוונט,
מיט פֿינגער ווי ספֿירות, איבער מענטש און שטיין, —
ווערט יעדער שטיין — אַ חלום ווי יעקבס שטיין:
יעקבס לייטער, ווי דער הימל אַזוי נאָענט.
וויפֿל שויבן אַזוויפֿל זונען אין אָוונט.
פֿון אַ שטיין ווערט אַ מלאך, פֿון אַ מלאך — אַ שטיין.
ווי אַ קוש פֿון גאָט, די קילקײַט פֿון אָוונט.
אַ צאַרט איז איצט אַפֿילו צאָרן, אַפֿילו שטיין.

EVENING IN SAFAD

Ari Hakodesh in the cool of evening,
with fingers like Sephiroth over man and stone,
turns each stone into a dream, like Jacob's stone,
Jacob's ladder as near as the sky.
There are as many suns as windowpanes.
A stone turns into an angel, an angel into a stone.
Like a kiss of God is the cool of evening.
O tender is now even scorn, even stone.

Translated by Rivke Katz

EDITOR'S NOTE: Ari Hakodesh/Isaac Luria (1534-1572), founder of the *Practical Kabbalah,* was born in Jerusalem to Ashkenazi parents. In this system of mysticiam, he suggested that *Kavvanah* (intense mental concentration) is capable of bringing man to a closer understanding of God and Creation. He also advanced the doctrine of transmigration of souls. His pupils and colleagues regarded him as the forerunner of the Messiah, as a performer of miracles, and named him the *Ari* (Lion) *Ha-Kodesh,* initials of three Hebrew words signifying the "Ashkenazi Rabbi Isaac" with the attribute "The Holy." In the latter part of his life, he settled in Safad, the center of the study of Kaballah, where he died and is buried. Menke was a practicing Kabbalist. He wrote *Tsfat,* the collection from which these Yiddish poems were taken, in a hut facing the grave of the Ari Hakodesh.

בימי הגשמים

גוט וואָס פֿאַרגאַנגען איז שוין דער זומער, זאַט אין שיינקייט,
בײַם גליענדיקן טײ איז אַ ליבער גאַסט דער טרויער.
גוט וואָס דער חלום קען אַ הויקער אויף אַ קרוין בײַטן.
גוט איז ווינטער אין צפת זײַן דער מלך פֿון טרויער.

וואָלקנס קומען אין צפת אַזוי נאַענט, אַזוי אייגן,
ווי זיי וואָלטן מער צו דער ערד, ווי צום הימל געהערט.
וואָלקנס ווי אַלטיטשקע אויף שטעקנס געבויגן,
קומען ווי פֿון גן-עדן אַ האַרך טאָן נײַעס אויף דער ערד.

לכבֿוד די לאַנג דערוואַרטע געסט, די געבענטשטע רעגנס,
שפּיל איך אַדעם צו דער בענקשאַפֿט אויף דער מאַנדעלינע.
די טעג קומען אומזיסט אויף אַ שטראַלעכל זיך פֿרעגן.
דער ווינט דורך די נעכט — אַ הײזעריקע קאַטערינקע.

רעגנס פֿלאַפּלען, ווי פֿון דרימל, לאַנג פֿאַרגעסענע רייד.
אין אויוון בלויז בלויט אַ פֿלאַם, אַ שטיק האָפֿערדיקער הימל.

RAINY DAYS IN SAFAD

Good the summer has gone by sated with beauty,
Solitude is a welcome guest at the glowing tea.
Good the dream can change a hunchback into a crown.
Winter. Good to be in Safad, king of solitude.

Clouds come to Safad so close as if of your own kin,
as if they belonged more to the earth than to the sky,
come like oldsters bent on walking sticks as from Eden.
They are all ears to hear news on earth.

To honor the long-awaited guests, the blessed rains,
I play odes to the wistful on the mandolin.
Days ask in vain if there is still some summer left.
The wind through the nights is like a hoarse organ grinder.

Rains chatter as if out of slumber long-forgotten chats.
The blue flame in the stove is like a fragment of hopeful sky.

Translated by Rivke Katz and the author

צפת

צפת, קרוין
פֿון גליל,
מיט געסעלעך
פֿון דורות דלות
אויסגעקרימט, פֿון חכמה
און די טריט פֿון משיח
אויסגעקאַרבט. באַרוועסע בעטלער
זײַנען דאָ די ערשטע צו טאָג,
אַנטקעגן אַ הימל, נאָענט ווי דער
גן־עדן וואָס אר״י הקדוש האָט דאָ
אויף שטיין און דאַרן פֿאַרפֿלאַנצט. אַ ווען איך זע די זון
אין וואונדער איבער וואונדערער שטאַרבן, דאַן ווייס איך אַז
שיין ווי דו קען זײַן אַפֿילו דער טויט, הער איך דעם ווינט
שווערן אַז מײַן פֿאָלק איז אייביק, ווי רבי עקיבֿא
דורך אײַזערנע קאַמען, ווי דײַן הימל וואָס וועט דאָ
קיינמאָל ניט אויפֿהערן בלויען. די לעגענדעם
שמעקן דאָ מיט ריחות פֿון אונדזער פֿאַסטעך —
שטאַם. אַז לעבן איז אייביק, דערצײַלן
באַגינענס, צפת, שוועסטער פֿון פֿלאַקער
וואָס ווערט קיינמאָל ניט פֿאַרברענט. גאָט
איז פֿון דײַן בין־השמשות
לערנען שיין צו שטאַרבן
און גוט איז פֿון דײַן
פֿאַרטאָג לערנען
זיך אייביק
לעבן.

SAFAD

Safad,
crown of the
Galilee with
alleys crooked as
the ages of the poor,
wrinkled by wisdom, echoed
by steps of Messiah. Barefoot
beggars are the first here to dawn at
a sky as near as Eden which Holy
Ari planted here on stone and thorn. My hymn
to your skies for giving my love a shade of your
blue. Safad, when I see your sunsets die in wonder
over wonder, I know wondrous as you may be even
death. I hear winds swear, my people are infinite as Rabbi
Akiba, embraced by God when grated by the Romans
with iron combs. Legends are scented here with fragrance
of the Song of Songs, with aeons of our shepherd
tribes. (Ask any dream if life is eternal.)
Safad, sister of the Burning Bush, good
to learn of your twilights to die like
Moses, handsome as the Book of
Splendor. Good to learn of your
dawns to live forever
and ever and a
Wednesday. And say
ye Amen.
Selah.

Translated by Menke Katz

A YIDDISH POET

I am a Yiddish poet—a doomed troubadour,
a dreamsmith jeered by the soft-voiced yokel,
the smooth snob with the swinging lash shrieking: jargon!
O are the mocked tears of my people a jargon?

Yiddish,
formed as Adam of the dust of the four corners of the earth;
the quenchless blaze of the wandering Jew,
the thirst of the deserts.

My mother tongue is unpolished as a wound, a laughter,
   a love-starved kiss,
yearnful as a martyr's last glance at a passing bird.
Taste a word, cursed and merciless as an earthquake.
Hear a word, terse and bruised as a tear.
See a word, light and lucent, joyrapt as a ray.
Climb a word—rough and powerful as a crag.
Ride a word—free and rimeless as a tempest.

Yiddish,
The bare curse thrown against the might of pitiless foes.
A "black year" shrouding dawn after a massacre.
The mute call of each speechless mouth of Treblinka.
The prayer of stone to turn into gale.

HYMN TO THE POTATO

O my first hymn was to the potato,
lure of my childhood, fruit of the humble,
the diurnal festival of the poor.

No fruit is noble as the potato.
Cherries are coy, plums have hearts of true stone.
The wind is a drunk fiddler at the grape.

The potato knows how much light there is
in the fertile darkness of seeded earth,
kissing the dust to which Adam returned.

On the hungry alleys of my childhood,
the Milky Way was a potato land.

GOLD DIGGERS

Michalishek, village of my mighty
ancestors, bearded rivermen reared in woods,
with the chilled iron of axes in their glance,
foil the foe gnawing the root in its crib,
wean the saplings in their tree nurseries,
towing barges, drive onward to Eden:
Yiddish flowing as the Viliya river,
biting as the coarse teeth of a ripsaw.
Earthbred, illstarred gardeners with lucky spades,
digging potatoes like buried treasures,
gold diggers with potato forks ransack
the furrows stabbed with daggers of broken rock;
the potatoes—tricksters, play hide and coop,
in the tired earth of Lithuania.

A flock of roaming goats frolic around
the hekdesh where the beggars, the feeble,
the chronic derelicts loiter, grazing
the straw roofs blended with duff and leafmold,
hit by the evil eye of goat suckers;
the he-goats: whiskered, entranced goat-gods
gallop at midnight, in illuminous
ecstasy when terrorized by a falling
meteor, a mortal from Paradise,
a fugitive from the night sky, breaking
away from the chains of infinity,
bringing the twisted lanes into the
solar ranks as if dilapidated
Pig Street and the seventh heaven are one.

Eden on Fridays is always nearby.
Angels visit here like next door neighbors,
assert that Elijah is on the way,
with the Sabbath feast for the sabbathless poor.
Badane, mother of a craving fivesome,
depends neither on angels nor Elijah,

but on the miracle of her skilled hands
which pick the wood-sorrel, the berry-cone,
garlic, the pride of the lily family;
lentils, the value of Esau's birthright,
sauce sweetened and stewed to a goody pulp,
the keen aroma of cool ciderkin,
made of the tasty refuse of apples,
of rootstock, the seed, stem and skin of the grape.

If not challahs fit for a silver wedding,
a roll, by the grace of blessed candlelight,
with a scent of honey for the Sabbath queen.
If not gefilte fish stuffed with savored crust,
a herring, humble as fresh waters, spawning
in sod huts, legends of the North Atlantic.
Mead (call it wine with a raw grain of salt)
served in laurel pink goblets from pitchers
born by the hands of village potters, with
ears and lips of clay licking yeast, honey malt,
adorned through ghost-fire in underglazed colors,
stored in dark cellars to drink l'chaim
to each breath of every creature on earth,
at the light of the long zero winter.

Children in the rapture of reveries
see their father Heershe Dovid in far
America, mining the gold of the silks
fondled in the factories of New Jersey.
The hekdesh turns into a castle of gold.
Elchik leads the human wreckage into
a world baked like a round kugel, the moon
of yogurt, the stars—crisp potato balls.
Berke rides a bear made of prime confetti.
Menke sees Jonah in the kind whale, welcomed
with milk and honey. Yeiske is about
to reach the sun as a plum of bonbon.
Bloomke, the only sister, cries over
spilled milk of crushed almonds, to nurse her

pampered doll made of the sweets of marzipan.
O the dream is swifter than the wind, it brought
America into Michalishek.

Heaven on earth is in the children's eyes.
Who is richer in gold, America
or the sun? Elchik says: at dawn, the sun
is richer, at twilight, America.
Berke tells of a street—a dream in New York,
paved with silver dollars like little moons.
Menke in heder confides, his father
Heershe Dovid (tall, yearning and handsome)
sailed the seas to change his jaded horse
for a gallant filly, the squeaking wagon,
for a two-wheeled pleasure carriage; to trade
the cow with the drying udders, hardly
enough for milksnakes—for a herd of an
aristocratic breed with teats like milkwells.
Sunset. Yeiske sees the clouds sail like boats
with gold which dad sent from America.
Bloomke fears there may be a shipwreck in
the clouds and flood the village with gold.

O the singing Jews of Michalishek:
O my unsung uncles, gloried horseshoers,
famed to shoe horses as they leap off the ground.
Jews with bodies like wrought metal; hammers
pride their hands over the anvils; felling
trees, hewing timber: robust, manful lovers,
lure the longing mermaids out of their streams,
to break their mirrors into dazzling charms,
to languish lovemad at their feet, to pine away.
on the mudlands of the Viliya river.

PRINCES OF PIG STREET

September is as rich as King Midas.
The winds which shake the summer off a birch
remain with the curse of a golden touch;
as if the village cannot live without
the yearning of want it trades its prosperous
colors for the hue and clamor of the
moaning charlatans—the criers of autumn
which bring December in as a frozen ghoul.
Blackbirds cross the village to proclaim ill fate.
The owls in empty barns hoot disaster.
Mother Badane hears a suspicious rumor
in every breeze: Germans, Russians, both foes,
prowl through the forest of Zaborchi,
both victors count each other's carrions,
both fatten the naked heads of vultures.
Her lucky children, the princes of Pig Street:
Elchik, Berke, Menke, Bloomke, Yeiske,
still find crumbs of bread in the breadless basket,
their skullcaps adorned like crowns, in gaberdines,
woolen boots, winterbound, wealthy with the
dugout treasures of legends. Bloomke, their only
ever-blushing sister, her cheeks glowing
like apples of Sodom, kneads of the first snow
a laughing milkmaid, milking in two pails,
the snow like flakes of milk from the sky.

Still, as if some mystic command stopped every breath
silence is a dumb, deaf and mute dragon.
Hush-sh-sh-sh, who is the strange horseman lurking
through the starry solitude of the village?
With one hand he guides his obedient
horse, with the other—the loaded carbine,
about to explode the calm of ages.
Each shadow resembles a Russian bear.
Vigilant: he is all-ear, all-eye.

Selah, the deadman's dog, believed to be
of the celestial hierarchy,
the friend of the dead, drowsing at the
crumbling gate of the ancient cemetery,
suddenly awakes barking at the intruder
all the curses of the valley of Hinnom
(which Amy the sorceress claims as her
private property). O who would dare to
penetrate here the eternal night,
if not Satan in his ecstasy of sin?

Beilichke, the legendary whore or saint
of the village, the walking doll of Pig Street,
lures the German armies away like Joan of Arc.
Her body is in itself a blond market.
She is from head to toes—vendable charm.
Her flirting arse is worth a loaf of bread,
an enchanted slap and a soldier's kiss.

Fire! Horses groan in burning stables.
A Bible burns in limbo like a
flying firebush, appealing to the merciful
and to the sons of the merciful.
In ashes of sepher-torahs sits Adonoi,
a black billet. Tongues of fire lick
a friendly wolf out of Isaiah's dream,
as it carries to safety a baby lamb.

A brave calf consoles a frightened lion:
"Brother, do not fear the angel of death.
We are all on our way to Paradise."
The little child leading us all since Adam
to the end of time storms God off his throne:
Help O help, king of the universe,
but lo, God cries for help to the little child.

Jesus in a blazing church, horror-stricken,
seeking a savior through the savage heavens.
Itche the convert, wearing one feminine,

one masculine shoe, kicks the devil out
of the hallowed ashes of his fallen Lord:
No, not the Lord fell, it is the fall of man
he sees baptized through fire, blood, dust.
He orders Yoorke the godsmith to weld
a new Jesus. He sees the souls of
the village hover in wind, hiding
in the fissures of uprooted tombstones,
in fear of Eden for even the Lord is on fire.
He hears heaven and earth, God's firstborn children
praying to Moloch for entrance to Gehenna.

Left of Pig Street is the wicked wonder
of flying roofs. The splintered houses form
ashen garlands, darken the light of
every prayer, remind there was once
a wistful alley there. The mudbank soiled
with bloodlust reminds there were once
people here. The shattered windows
saw a thousand times a thousand suns rise and fall here.

IN ABANDONED BARRACK

Dveirke,
Dveirele,
Oi, Dveirinke!
loveliest of bare
foot girls bred on the poor
soil of einkorn wheat, flailed grain,
lilac blue, potato apples.
I write these lines yearning for you in
this abandoned barrack which is stained with
the death of German and red armies who bled
here white; mad with longing, high fever and hounding
whims, left alone to fight fancymongers, a sunset
or two before I die. The winds are here to curse my last
twilights. The late sun is a snowrose in the teeth of the frost.

DVEIRKE'S VOICE FROM THE WATERFALL

Elchik,
Elinke,
for you the light
of my blond braids, the
blossoms of my every
June. O hear the laughter of
the waterfall rout the cries of
the centuries! O leap into the
waterfall, into me, to fall without
a bruise over these hanging cliffs: half lions,
half eagles, griffins guarding the gold of sunsets.
Age in, age out (out of reach of death) scour blood, fear, guts,
humanize the sword, until it may cut the bread of God's
children. The dream, my love, is more real than all realities.

ON THE DEATH OF A DAY-OLD CHILD

All dead, day-old children will welcome you.
The wind will sing my lullabies to you,
when the sun falls where the saddest grass grows.

You are the beginning when light is wise.
God will guard to the end of days your day,
in the land of manna, Eden of bread.

With ray and shade you will play pranks all day.
Autumn will teem with the brown of your eyes.
With my grief will forever weep the dew.

HOMELESS CHILDREN

O homeless children
with the scorched look of burning
villages, in the giant

uniforms of dead
bolsheviks, like dusty toy
soldiers, rise against

God demanding life,
in the dumps of Pig Street. O
they scare the blues out

of the April skies,
loiter through twisted alleys
with the twilight bats.

O the waifs and strays,
closed buds growing underfoot,
folks rumor their cries

deafen the ears of
the scant breadgrains, darken the
translucent kernels

of the durum Spring-
wheat, leaving only in the
crippled fields—glume blotch.

OLD MANHATTAN

Sundown. God, I am lonely, I will go
to the whorealleys of old Manhattan
and fetch me a jolly liberal bride.

The evening is drunk with its own wine on
our wedding bed, you will be my wife an hour,
I, your lover—a thousand and one nights.

I am all yours, my unmothered, unowned love:
I swear by the ecstasy of our trance,
by the hatched shadowbands of this twilight.

Night bears the commerce of licensed kisses,
the law-ridden guardians of humdrum,
bereaved of you and me, of our soulquake.

You left, O firefooted elf of the streets.
The summer, greensick, cankers on cracked walls.
Flowers in a pot pine for home—the far fields.

My bride coquets through the blight of slummed streets:
wholesale dealers in smoke, iron, gold, death,
praying through the ages for their downfall.
Even time is tired here of night and day.

ON PIMPS

Pimps will never die.
They sneak out of hell to lure
the nine orders of
angels into their under-
ground brothels of all heavens.

Eve in their hands is
a nude whore who never tires
shouting bargains to
the resurrected dead: two
bits for a heavenly screw.

AT A PATCHED WINDOW

I am a lover, a pauper, and a poet.
My heart is clean beneath the threadbare shirt.
I learned wisdom from the talmudic skies of Lithuania.
I am gracefully uncouth.
I cleaved my grace from the slums of New York.

My father like Columbus dreamed of America, when I was born.
My childhood waned at a patched window,
where I imagined a cake soaring like a cherub,
where I saw candy, toys, and cocoa,
under the wings of a nymph only.

The cruel hand of destiny led us through hunger, war, and plague.
We were four little brothers and a scrawny sister.
In the autumn garret we heard the song of spring,
as crawling doves would hear the giggle of their craven victor.
The wind through redolent meadows was a bleak laughter.

O our weary mother carried us
through the prosperous thorns of our scared little town, Michalishek.
From a fairy tale came the night—a spectral undertaker,
to bury the thorny day of Lithuania.
God was the baker from Eden who baked the tasty stars.

ISAIAH ON FREEDOM

Isaiah is always there
where builders build a new jail.
He says: Alas, my grim sons,
the sword is still not a plow.
If one image of God will
be somewhere chained in a cell
the chain will shackle us all,
in heaven and on earth.
Angels will know the weight of
the chain, winds will not be free
to curse even their own fate.
The sky will be an endless
prison roof if one captive
will still remain in a cell,
at the end of time, nearby.

FIRST POET

God, the first poet, created worlds out of words
as the last poet will at the end of love
and hate, tears and laughter, good and evil.
God, overblessed, driven through prayer
mills, overbored with man and beast,
angel and archfiend, he will
return heaven and earth
to pre-genesis,
beyond space, time:
to tohu-
bohu.

ON THE BIRTH OF ELOHIM

First there was the dream, before time, before God was born.
(Ask a speck of dust how old are Adam and Eve.)
Dream is en-sof—infinity. You, I and
no one were in tohu-bohu, waiting
for heaven, earth. We were the void-end
like God craving for birth. A void
struck a void, there was first spark,
Zohar, child of light brought
the sun, stirred in space
a still small voice:
Elohim.

FROM THE TREE OF KNOWLEDGE

My son, learn to love
solitude like God before
he created time,
the fate of man: Job and boils
and the island universe.

Learn philosophy
from a wounded wolf, howling
to God and the stars.
Learn to meditate from old
gravestones, moss-crowned, muse-ridden.

SIDE AND MIDDLE THOUGHTS

When Eve the first bride on earth lay nude to make love
with Adam her newlyborn bridgroom, he loved
only her side rib out of which she was
made, it was all his own. She was lured
to his enchanted middle horn.
She said: stab me, my love, in
the middlepit. He thought
her middle thrill is
God, leading Cain,
Abel, Seth:
mankind.

ON ADAM

Adam was not chased
out of Eden, he escaped
like a convict out
of the sight of God to be
free as Satan in hell.

Adam
will return
to Eden when
the blessed wrecker will
raze the grief of the last
jail on earth. O see the sun:
a clock which tells of a dawn when
the last doomed will outdevil death and
let the cheated hangman hug the gallows.

LILITH

Lilith will be the
last whore on earth, the last life
of the last race. She
will rape God, will give birth to
heavenless, bastard angels.

MARUSAH
(twin sonnet)

Winter.
Night. Hoarfrost.
The village is
drowned in sleep. Who, if
not Marusah, the sleep
walker would walk out of her
dreams, seeking her lover, hugging
the goblet where wine, vows and blood were
mixed in a toast to their eternal love?
She sees the houses turn into iceborn bears,
the chimneys—snow-eagles, eager to seize, tear their
prey. Led by the moon she walks over the roofs through an
invisible fire which neither life nor death may quench. The
stars (the wise, overworked clichés) are gems out of Satan's crown.

What is left of her lover in this winter-worn village if
not a luring icicle on the eaves of the tranced roof
(erect as an ice-penis raping a star), which she
licks as a drink offering to love, until it
is a horn of a musk ox piercing her fate,
until she is found—a frozen Venus,
under her unlucky star. Dawn. Clouds:
woolly mammoths carry her like
gold to the devil's treasure;
winds rush to clip their tusks,
to build ivory
castles where she
still dreams, pines,
yearns, loves.

ON THE SINS OF GOD

God of mercy, are you not merciless to turn into dust
your own image to place as guards the Cherubim and the
flaming sword, to keep Eden locked, to create hell in
heaven after hell on earth for the only sin
of tasting one of your all-wise apples? (Fit
for a miser, hoarder of apples.) King
of the universe, would it not be
just to lead yourself through all the
torments of Gehenna to
atone for your wrongs since
Adam, until man
of true mercy
will forgive
your sins?

QUEENS OF AUTUMN

Yeah, old
women are
the true queens of
autumn as they see
their twilights turn into
starlight. Crickets serenade
their wistful evenings. Old women
are comeliest when dressed in the full
glory of the autumn colors. Their walk
is beautiful among goldenrods with stems
like wands, carried by elves, dolled for the jubilees
of their diamond weddings. Even May is a cousin
of autumn. The buzz of hungry bees reminds of a lost
lover. They hear his voice in the song of the oriole, his
nectar still on their tongues is enough to fill with honey the
cup and saucer vine. They see faded blossoms bud into
seed again. Their memories scent of meadow-saffron.
Their fingers are queenly in white, green or purple
sapphires. Days gather like birds in restless flocks
ready to migrate. It is good to die
in May when cushions of grass and beds
of dandelions grow best, their blind
dates with fate, at sunset, is
all crystalline; rooted
in legends like gnarled
trees, bearing fruit
of a new
blest age.

MY SISTER BLOOMKE

My love-
lorn, widowed
sister, Bloomke,
learned to weep from the
weeping willows: silent
mourners born at the longing
bank of the Viliya river
which hugged the village, its bosom friend,
night and day around its hoarse cuckoo clocks.
The weeping willows prospered until they reached
the patched windowholes of the house where she was born.
She learned hospitality from the willows as they
gave their generous shade to weary beggars who wandered
ages through the bare distances of Lithuania, gaunt
paupers, rich with the crumbs of kindly bread in their beggar bags
always ready to share their wealth with birds, mice, fish in the
lucky waters of the village where her forefathers
nourished centuries of love, hate, fought wolves in the
wild forests, kicked the noble guts out of the
robber barons, laughed, cried, died, leaving their
widows look at the black tails of the
widow-birds like veils, famishing
the light of withered summers.
She saw the first budbreak
commune with the end,
with the fallen
star, with the
blindworm.

MY UNCLE BENTKE, PRINCE OF CARDS

Crown of my family tree on the magic carpet of cards.
Your servants were kings, queens who reigned under you: fate gambler.
The sun rose and fell in your royal flush of poker.
Cards laugh, cry, love, hate. Cards—gifts of the gods, dreamers
found treasures hidden in rich dreams. Cards—dreamboats
sailed through never-seas where aces ruled life
and death. Goddesses of fate obeyed
your command to load with fire, brim
stone, even your dud cards, to
destine for poker-faced
hicks, cards like deathbells,
ring downfall. O
wizard of
wizards!

Bentke, eighty-year-old prankster, what can you do in heaven,
if not tickle pink the angels until they are laughing jack
asses, play pinochle with seraphim as they guard
God's throne, win all the stars until the heavens are
blind and you play solitaire in limbo when
kicked out of hell. Come O come Bentke, I
hear the winds shuffle your nights and days
like packs of cards, each card dreams of
your wondrous fingertips as
a sleeping beauty of
the touch of her prince
charming in an
enchanted
castle.

SNOWFALL IN THE VILLAGE OF MICHALISHEK

Children in my dream-
ful village saw in a snow
fall the celestial
hierarchy fall, every
snowflake—a fallen angel.

Some flakes were seraphs,
some cherubs, some archangels.
Snow brought the crooked
alleys into heaven. Each
snowflake left a tear for the

poor synagogue mouse
and a kiss of peace
for the dust of the
nearby cemetery, the
Eden of my forefathers.

SNOWFALL IN BOROUGH PARK

Snowfall.
Borough Park
eats all its dumps
away. The crooked
roof of a poet's dream-
attic is like a hanging
garden of Babylon. Diseased
fruits, resting in the gutter, on their
way to hell, are in full blossom again.
A mouse—a homeless ghost, queen of the wretched
with a crown of snowgems, wrought by God's personal
jewelsmith, runs to safety from its enemy light to
its only friend—darkness; walled-in phantoms, petting their snow
beards, amuse it with the brightest gloom in newborn Borough Park.

AT A CUP OF COFFEE
to Yeiske

I write these lines to
you, unpolished as your name,
unmeasured as love.
My private island is a
table in a coffee shop.

Just an hour sojourn,
in self-served meridian
splendor. I daydream
safaris on dazed camels.
Broadway is a crude cart road.

The safaris crushed
on rock, skull and cliff of the
nerve-ridden city;
echoed and re-echoed through
the hoarse air of Manhattan.

A cup of coffee
is my shield. A trance
eludes the jam on Times Square.
It is coffeetime—chat time,
from dawn to dawn in New York.

O the humble joy
of a cafeteria,
detouring hell with
you and glowing friends at a
cup of coffee—cup of dreams.

AGAINST LOCK OR RHYME

Poems,
sit in rhymes
like men, birds, beasts
in cages. I saw
Samson with fist in the
teeth of a lion forced to
his knees under the load of rhymes.

Poet,
brother, let
your word roll un
rhymed as thunder, let
it flash like free lightning
through the fog: over a parched
field, the eager harbinger of
rain. The poem in rhyme bends like a
captured enemy under an arched yoke.
A chased deer, in panic, through the forest does
not race in rhyme, a grieved stone does not mourn in rhyme.
The rhyme, patted, rounded by the file of crystal verse,
cuts into the flesh of a word like a wound. If like thirst,
stream, sun, storm is eternal the poem, lock not the storm in
the cell of a rhyme. Give the word the fresh scent of ripe corn,
swaying in wind of a hopeful field, tasty as rare
bread of my hungry childhood. Let the word ride on,
speak face to face with your neighbor of a far
century. Wars do not kill in rhyme. A
plummeting airplane like a wounded
eagle does not fall in rhyme. A
hurricane does not uproot
trees in rhyme. A stormy
sea is a rhymeless
call for a day
without lock
or rhyme.

BEYOND ALL BEYONDS

I will learn from stones the language of silence.
On a bare field, I will be an empty
pod dreaming of lost blossoms of gone-
by summers. A last autumn fly
straying through its night of doom
will touch me like darkness,
to share the end-all,
as if it were
the last life
on earth.

Mine will be heaven and earth. Winter brooks
under ice will rush me to the first
beginning, beyond all beyonds.
I will hear seeds fight for life
in the womb of the earth.
In an injured haw-
thorn, I will smart
like a wound,
like hope.

The last hour like the first is all wonder
like the opening of infant buds of
marsh marigolds. Each dusk embraces
dawn: an eternal love in life
as well as in death, through rise
and fall of ages. O
my love, let us not
lose a trice of
the marvels
of death.

MY LAST POEM

This is my last poem, a death-bell each rhyme.
All the days are locked, the key thrown away.
When I reach the last line is the end of time,
the end of life and death of night and day.

These last words as condemned steps to gallows lead.
The sun—a golden noose in hangman's hand.
Beyond me, glowing, furrow-cloven, I leave
in lone metaphors my women stranded,

sensuous, longing for my manful touch in vain.
Women I know from a hundred years hence,
yearning for me as parched soil for plough and rain,
wave hands of tomorrow to my last glance.

The end ends at the beginning, before birth,
before ghost and ghoul, before heaven and earth.

MY LAST PRAYER

Evening. The sun falls
as under a guillotine.
Thank you God that I
see my last sunset, that I
now turn into grass, stone, night.

O lead me beyond
the first or last life on earth,
beyond the unborn.
O thank you God that I will
still be in every rainbow.

EPITAPH

I am the lover
who drowned in the Viliya
river, swimming to
my love with a Forget-Me-
Not flower yearning in my hand.

ABOUT THE AUTHOR

Menke Katz was born June 7, 1906, in Shvintsian, and grew up in Michalishek, shtetls in Lithuania. In 1920, he emigrated to the United States where he quickly mastered English. He started writing poetry in English but quickly turned back to Yiddish, the mameloshn, the language of his family and birthplace. He attended Columbia University, 1924-26; the University of Southern California, 1926-27; and later, Brooklyn College, 1946-48. In all, he authored some eighteen books. Nine of these were in Yiddish, including: *Drei shvester* (Three Sisters), 1932; *Der mentch in togn* (Dawning Man), 1935; *Brenendik shtetl* (Burning Village), two volumes, 1935; *S'hot dos vort mayn bobe Moyna* (My Grandma Myrna Speaks), 1939; *Tsu dertsayin in freydn* (A Story to Be Told in Happier Days), 1941; *Der posheter cholem* (The Simple Dream), 1947; *Inmitn tog* (Midday), 1954; and *Tsfat* (Safad), 1979, the first part of which is included in this chapbook. Nine were in English, including: *Land of Manna*, 1965; *Rockrose*, 1970; *Burning Village*, 1972; *Two Friends* (with Harry Smith), 1981; *A Chair for Elijah*, 1985; *Two Friends II* (with Harry Smith), 1988; *Nearby Eden*, 1990. All of these books were poetry, except for a short-story collection, *Forever and Ever and a Wednesday*, 1980. He has also translated Hebrew writings of Rashi into English and Yiddish and has contributed, among others, to *The Atlantic Monthly, The New York Times, Commentary, Sewanee Review* and *Prairie Schooner*. His own work has been translated into nearly fifty languages to date. He also edited *Bitterroot*, an international little poetry magazine, the 100th issue of which was at press just before he died on April 24, 1991. And, on March 14, 1991—just six weeks before—along with the work of two other Jewish poets, Aaron Kramer and Gabriel Preil, his poetry was featured at the Dag Hammarskjöld Auditorium of the United Nations. He is survived by his second wife, Rivke, their son, Heershe-Dovid, his daughter by his first wife, Troim Handler, two granddaughters, and two great-grandchildren. *This Little Land*, 1992, is a selection of Menke's poetry. He considered himself to be a Yiddish poet, "a doomed troubadour," but his work will live on and continue to inspire his readers as long as there is a civilization . . . forever and ever and a Wednesday.

ABOUT THE TRANSLATORS AND ARTISTS

Rivke Katz was born and raised in the Borough Park section of Brooklyn, where she lived with Menke, and their son, Heershe-Dovid, for several decades until retiring to Spring Glen, a village in the Catskills. After earning her B.A. degree at Brooklyn College, she continued her studies at Hunter, City College, New York University, Columbia University, and the University of Colorado. She received art scholarships to Pratt Institute and the Brooklyn Museum Art School. For a number of years, she taught and coordinated various art programs in the New York City school system. Since Menke would not translate himself, she sometimes translated his Yiddish poetry into English. She also served as art editor of *Bitterroot* throughout its 100 issues and had several shows exhibiting her drawings and paintings.

Aaron Kramer first won national attention for *Seven Poets in Search of an Answer*, 1944, and *Poetry and Prose of Heinrich Heine*, 1948. He later produced, with twelve artists, *The Tune of the Calliope*. This was followed by *Rumshinsky's Hat*, 1964, *On the Way to Palermo*, 1973, and *Carousel Parkway*, 1980. Aside from Heine, his translations include: *Rosenfeld: The Teardrop Millionaire*, 1955; *Rilke: Visions of Christ*, 1967; and *The Emperor of Atlantis*, a deathcamp opera which premiered at the San Francisco Operat in 1977. His scholarly works include *The Prophetic Tradition in American Poetry*, 1968, and *Melville's Poetry*, 1972. A professor of English at Dowling College since 1961, Dr. Kramer also co-edits *West Hills Review: a Whitman Journal*.

Bebe Barkan, a native of Brooklyn, is a graduate of Hunter College. In addition to designing and illustrating books, she paints, designs textiles, creates wearable art, and produces soft sculptures. Currently, she is working as an attendance teacher in Queens. She lives with her poet-husband, Stanley H. Barkan, and their two children, Mia and Scott, in Merrick, New York, and frequently exhibits locally and internationally.